The World According to KIDS

For three remarkable teachers:

Will taught the value of laughter.
Lora taught the value of knowledge.
Helen taught the value of dedication.

All knew the value of love.

The World According to KIDS

Compiled by
Harold Dunn

Illustrated by
HOWARD MUNCE

SPECTACLE LANE PRESS

Published by Spectacle Lane Press
Box 34, Georgetown, CT 06829
ISBN 0-930753-11-9

Published simultaneously in the United States and Canada.
Printed in the United States of America.

INTRODUCTION

Have you heard that a bunkhouse is where cowboys go to tell how brave they are and other such bunk? Or that the ash around volcanoes was once hot java? That *double jeopardy* means being arrested by two *jeopardy* sheriffs? Or that a baby born today can expect to have a longer *gevity* than his parents?

I'm personally acquainted with the eager young students who were once positive about these off-center bits of information. I was their teacher.

Before I retired after teaching for 32 years, I collected their beguiling observations and found that youngsters often misinterpret just a word or two. But that's all it takes to cause a comical kind of chaos.

Here's a perfect example of a child's mind at work, trying to combine what the teacher said with what he is beginning to sense about the confusing world around him:

"Once there was this Nathan Hale who was a spy. But not an ordinary spy. He was a good one. Even when caught he knew he was right, so he died rather happily ever after."

The young writer had been taught that Nathan Hale had died gloriously and heroically. But he didn't quite understand what this meant, so he came up with that unique expression about "dying happily ever after."

I suspect that afterward the boy thought it over and hedged a little by saying that Hale died "rather" happily.

Children are constantly observing, thinking, and trying to put it all together. Much of the fun in talking with them comes from the startling way they can put a backspin on their answers, saying something that seems absurd to adults, yet sensible at the same time.

One snowy day I was on playground duty. As I struggled to put a pair of overshoes on a six-year-old boy, I remarked, "These overshoes are getting too small." But the lad shrugged his shoulders and patiently explained to me, "They're the same size they've always been."

During an Open House at our school, I heard one mother, trying to get her four-year-old daughter to eat her meal, say, " Susie, your peas are saying, 'Eat me! Eat me!'" The tiny girl stared at the peas and slowly picked up her fork. As she methodically began mashing each one, she muttered, "Shut up, peas!"

I've always thought that the humor of childhood is the funniest kind because it's so honestly spontaneous and truly human, and I continually found examples of childhood wisdom as well as laughter. Together, the wit and wisdom provide illuminating insight into the way children look at our world.

Harold Dunn
Ballwin, Missouri

TABLE OF CONTENTS

QUIXOTIC Q&A

Question: Were there many forms of life in the Paleozoic Era?

Answer: I don't know and Grandpa says he can't remember.

Question: How did the Paleozoic Era end?

Answer: A little at a time.

Question: What ruler reformed the Athenian government by devising juster laws?

Answer: Juster The First.

Question: How would Hercules fare against one of our modern heavyweight boxers?

Answer: Hercules would be so old he would get beat up easy.

Question: How does mechanical energy change into electrical energy?

Answer: By being a miracle.

Question: When were the Middle Ages?

Answer: Somewhere around 40.

Question: What was Washington's reply to Cornwallis' surrender ultimatum?

Answer: Something smart.

Question: Who said, "Give me liberty or give me death"?

Answer: Patrick Henry something. I forget his last name.

Queston: What is a boom town?

Answer: A town settled by Daniel Boom.

Question: Where are the seeds of the okra plant found?

Answer: At Hardy's seed store.

Question: What are the three main parts of an insect?

Answer: Interior, exterior and posterior.

Question: What does FF in music mean?

Answer: Hold your ears.

Question: Define syncopation.

Answer: Syncopation is not just boom boom. It is boom ba da boom or sometimes boom ca pa doodle da rest boom boom.

Question: As the tubing in a trombone is lengthened, why is the pitch lowered?

Answer: I explained this to the science teacher last week. Check with him for the right answer.

Question: Who composed The Hallelujah Chorus?
Answer: God.

Question: Name an animal peculiar to the Australian continent.

Answer: It would be peculiar to see a polar bear there.

Question: What kind of songs did Franz Schubert compose?
Answer: Good ones.

Question: What did Robert Schuman become when he grew up?
Answer: Leonard Bernstein.

Question: What are two laws that govern the use of money?

Answer: Don't steal it and keep it moving.

Question: Give two examples of secret societies in our own culture.

Answer: Republicans and Presbyterians.

Question: What is one of our chief imports from Canada?

Answer: Coldness.

Question: Why do compasses always point north?

Answer: They are stubborn that way.

Question: What might we expect to find at the bottom of a lake?

Answer: Stuff.

Question: What is the modern geological era called?

Answer: The modern geological era.

Question: Why does Brazil burn much of her coffee crop?

Answer: Because it smells so good when roasting.

Question: What does the phrase "splinter group" mean?
Answer: It means ouch!

Question: What is the president's Inaugural Address?
Answer: Somewhere on Pennsylvania Avenue.

Question: What does the inertial law of Galileo prove?
Answer: That there are some things I don't know.

Question: Why would a person weigh more at either pole than at the equator?
Answer: If you walk from either pole to the equator, you are bound to lose weight.

Question: What is the general shape of the earth?
Answer: Pretty bad.

Question: What happens to the ice in a glass of water?
Answer: The water eats it.

Question: When a glass is dropped, what causes it to break?
Answer: Carelessness.

Question: If you put the tip of a thermometer in boiling water, what would it say?

Answer: "Take me out!" if it could talk.

Question: Why is the flame extinguished when a bottle is placed over it?

Answer: Because of magic.

Question: What is the difference between a molecule and an atom?

Answer: A molecule is a little iddy biddy piece of a thing while an atom is a teensy weensy piece.

Question: In a free fall, how long would it take to reach the ground from a height of 2,000 feet?

Answer: I have never performed this experiment.

Question: What is the internationally used scientific system of measurement?

Answer: Hips, waist and bust.

Question: What does a falling barometer indicate?

Answer: That the law of gravity is still with us.

Question: What do stratus clouds look like?
Answer: Rain.

Question: Where is Mercury?
Answer: It hides in thermometers.

Question: Why is the sky blue?
Answer: Because when sunlight hits the air it bends a little, this being the right answer to one of the questions, this one I think.

Question: Why are days shorter in winter than in summer?
Answer: During the cold winter months the days get cold and contract. In the summer time they get hot and expand.

Question: Even on some clear nights we do not see all of the moon. Why not?
Answer: Because of invisible clouds.

Question: In what ways are we dependent on the sun?
Answer: We can always depend on the sun for tidal waves and sun burns.

WHO'S WHOM

Archimedes was a radical who said, "Give me a pole and a place to stand and I will move the world."

Aristides was called "The Just." No one ever said just what.

Irving Berlin wrote both the words and lyrics in his songs.

Daniel Boone was so good he could hit a target at 100 yards with one eye tied behind his back.

William Bryan was nominated for president in three different Democratic Convents.

James Buchanan was elected president even though he was accused of being a bachelor.

Julius Caesar was unscrupulous, scheming and a born leader of men.

Kit Carson was always fighting for peace with the Navajos.

Caruso was at first an Italian. Then someone heard his voice and said it would go a long way, so he came to America.

Sesqui Centennial is a famous 150-year-old Indian.

Grover Cleveland figured out how to be both our 22nd and our 24th president. He did it by getting beat by our 23rd president.

Agnus Dei was a woman composer famous for her church music.

Corpus Delicti was a famous lawyer, now dead.

Thomas Edison was considered a great inventor but we now know how many inventions he overlooked.

Euclid is one of the great figures of arithmetic. This figure looks something like a zero.

Vasco da Gama was a Portugoose discoverer. He discovered the Gama rays.

All stories have morals if we will just look for them hard enough. **Goldilocks** even taught me. She taught me not to eat other peoples' food or get in other peoples' beds.

It was **Nathan Haley** who said: "I only regret that I have but one life to lose for my country." This has come to be known as the famous Haley's comment.

Laissez-Faire was a Chinese economist.

Cyrus McCormick invented the grim reaper.

Plato was an astrologer who discovered a planet and named it after himself. Otherwise he was a fine Christian Gentleman who didn't believe in sin.

Sydney Porter wrote good short stories. He served a term in the pen. His pen name was O. Henry.

Pseudonym was a famous Greek poet.

Rousseau tries to tell everyone how to live. He thinks he's so smart. So pooey on Rousseau!

William Shakespeare was a very religious man because he wrote about Ye and Thee and people like that.

The abominable **Snowman** is called that because he won't let people shoot him.

So and So the Second is really So-and-So the Third because So-and-So, Jr. is second.

Socrates was a philosopher who always said No Thyself. You see he didn't believe he really existed.

Edmund Spenser wrote *The Faerie Queene* and was a wonderful writer despite his poor spelling.

Mark Twain, the humorist, changed his name because his mother named him Samuel Langhorne Clemens.

I have often wondered if Robin Hood and Riding Hood were relationed.

Whistler's was the dearest mother he had.

When all the votes were finally counted, it was found that **Woodrow Wilson** was only slightly elected.

It was **Wordsworth** who said "the child is father of the man." This was said in times before they knew as much as we do now.

WHIMSICAL WEBSTER

A

ABUNDANT
To desert, like he abundant his friends.

ACCOMMODATE
To do a person a favor whether he likes it or not.

ACCESSORY
Something to be worn around the neck, or help commit a murder. Sometimes both.

ACME
To be at the tippy tippy top. With an *n* instead of the *m* you only have pimples.

ADRIFT
What people do when they want to be alone and starve and die.

ALBATROSS
A good luck piece often hung around the neck.

AMBIDEXTROUS
Being able to throw either arm.

AMBIGUOUS The meaning is not clear.

AMOEBA A one-celled animal. But don't let him fool you. He has been around so long, some say he is the father of every living thing.

ANCESTOR An extinct relative.

APOLOGY Something a person says that he doesn't really mean.

ASTERISK A reminder to go look some place else if you want to know the whole truth.

B

BARBARISM The state or act of getting a haircut.

BIRD Anybody wanting to be a bird is not allowed to have teeth.

BOLD WEEVIL   Cotton growers must always watch out for attacks by the bold weevil.

C

CATS   They fly around with witches and have nine lives and are bad luck if they are black and that is all I know for sure about cats.

CHAISE   Like a chair except you look at it instead of sitting on it.

CHAPS   They are people if they are English. Or cowboys wear them around their legs.

CIRCLE   A straight crooked line.

CIRCUMFERENCE   Tells you how fat the circle is.

COMMAS   Used when you have to take a breath. Periods are used when you want to stop and think.

COMPLIMENT   To tell somebody
something that
isn't true.

CORONER   Someone who goes
around and decides
who looks like they
are dead.

COWBIRD   **I have never seen
one so I don't know
which is which half.**

CRUSTACEAN   This means you can
wear your bones on
your outside.

D

DACHSHUND A long-short body-legged dog.

DEAD RECKONING A method of finding out how long they have been dead.

DESPERATE When a person runs away just to keep from getting killed.

DIRGES Music written to be played at sad occasions, such as funerals, weddings and the like.

DUEL Music sung by two people at the same time.

DYNASTY A regenerating machine.

E

ECLAIRS Cookies with insides.

ENCORE What an audience gets if they are unruly.

ETCH   Where you need to scratch.

ETERNAL   Forever and maybe even longer.

F

FALL   When the leaves are no longer on tight.

FIGURE   What you write in arithmetic. Or walk with if you are a lady.

FOOT-POUNDS   How many you weigh if you are just standing on one foot.

FOREIGN LANGUAGE   Would be "bark! bark!" to a cat.

FORTISSIMO   Real loud. The way a composer yells on paper.

G

GELATIN   A sort of nervous.

GENETICS   Tells you how you got that way.

GYRO-STABILIZER   Used to help sea-sickness. But it hasn't completely replaced barfing.

H

HAMSTERS   They carry their meals in their pockets and their pockets in their cheeks.

HOBBY   Something a person enjoys doing that is none of his business.

HOMO SAPIENS   A group of animals just below the monkeys in intelligence.

HUMANITY   That part of us that is good but always getting into trouble.

I

IGLOO   A hut made of snow and ice. The Eskimos think it keeps them warm. They never learn.

IMMATURE	When you don't shave or have dates or even want to.
INCIDENT	Like an accident, only indoors.
INCONSISTENT	Means like tHiS.
INTROSPECTION	Looking within yourself. I have seen chickens do it at night.

J

JUNKET	A small pile of junk.

K

KNAPSACK	A bag you can take knaps in on camping trips.

L

LATIN	The language of the dead.
LEGATO	To sing it slow and make it sound like syrup.

LENT	A period of fast ones before Easter.
LOATH	Means reluctant and just by adding an "e" you can despise.

M

MARQUIS	A man that sticks out over theater doors. He is royalty so he can do it if he wants to.
MARTYR	A person that can't help from getting killed so he says he always wanted to anyway.
MICROSCOPE	Used to inspect things smaller than a naked eye.
MONSOON	A French gentleman.
MORRIS DANCE	A country dance from the time when people were happy.

N

NOM DE PLUME	The legal way to say "I don't have no feather!"

NUTHATCH	Most birds sit on eggs to hatch, but the nuthatch has other ideas.

O

OLIVES	Delicious unless you can't stand their taste.
OSTRICH	A queer-type bird that does not fly but runs like a horse. Except that he uses two legs which makes him a queer-type horse too.
OTTOMAN	A man with a low-cushioned seat.

P

PALETTE	A small friend.
PENTAGON	A six-sided general.
PLAINTIFF	The person on the guilty side.

PLUS   Two minuses make a plus. It's just one of those things.

POACH   To cook an egg in an illegal manner.

POIGNANT   How you get before the stork comes.

PRESENT   Right now. No it is too late. That present is past now. You have to look fast to see the present.

Q

QUADRUPED An animal with four pedigrees.

R

RACONTEUR A French racketeer.

REEDS   Little pieces of wood. They are found mostly in plants and clarinets.

REFRAIN	Means don't do it. A refrain in music is the part you better not play.
REPERTOIRE	The music a singer actually thought he could sing.
RITARDANDO	The music way of saying slow down and look out for what's up ahead.
REVERE	To daydream. But not the Paul kind of Revere.

S

SCALES	Found on snakes and pianos.
SELF-POLLINATING	A tree that is its own father.
SEPTUAGENARIAN	A person who knows how to have seven kids at once.

SERENE   Someone who doesn't realize how serious things are.

SESAME   A seed used for opening caves.

SEXTANT   I know what it is, but I would rather not say.

SHARK   A fish. You can tell by feeling its gills if you really want to know that bad.

SOIL   Helpful dirt.

SOLILOQUY   When someone starts talking to himself. It is o.k. if he does it while he is in a play.

SPRING   The way you can tell when it is here is to look for bears and birds flying backside from the south.

SQUARES	Circles with corners.
SYNTAX	A tax on things you aren't supposed to do anyway.

T

TEMPO	How fast people are singing when they can no longer be measured in miles per hour.
TIDES	They are very interesting if you happen to be interested in them.
TIMBERLINE	An altitude. Don't take anything made of wood above it, or else.
TROUBLE SHOOTER	An expert at ending it all.
TROUSSEAU	A pair of women's trousers.

TYKE	The son of a tycoon.

U

ULTIMATUM	The final offer that will be made until the next one.
UNICORN	A horsey animal with four feet and only one corn.
URANIUM	An active element in a radio.

V

VIBRATING	A vibrating thing is a thing that cannot make up its mind which way it wants to go.
VICE	Something bad like a vice president.

W

WAVE	When a wave rolls over on itself it is called a breaker. Of just about anything, I guess.
WHITE ELEPHANTS	Valuable stuffs of no worth.

X

X'S

Becoming close to extinct. Used mainly for signing and kissing.

Y

YEOMAN

A sort of yesman.

YODEL

A cry for help often heard in the Swiss Alps.

YOKE

The yellow of an egg put around the neck of an ox. Only the oxes know why.

Z

ZERO

Tells me to think of nothing.

ZIGZAG

A sideways flip flop.

THE PHARAOHS AND THEIR MOMMIES

While other creatures were just playing around and having a good time, mankind was hard at work thinking how to evolve.

What made the wheel so important as an invention is that it didn't just roll. It could also travel.

The first available records of Egypt have the date 5000 B.C. in them.

Algebraic was first spoken by the ancient Egyptians.

All the Pharaohs wanted to be mommies. It usually killed them.

After they died, the Pyramids were buried in their Pharaohs.

They made Socrates drink some poison hemlock even though a lot of them felt he was not really worthy of death.

Plato was a thinker who died in the year 347 and wasn't born until 427. He thought out how to do this.

People first shook hands to prove they had no arms. Except they could keep their flesh and boney kind.

At the conclusion of an event in the Greek Olympics a wraith was placed on the head of the winner.

The Athenians also called themselves Ionians and Greeks. This confused their enemies and made them think there were more of them.

Well-cooked meat was rare for the caveman.

The Greeks made Gods of the stars, the trees, the animals, the--well, nothing was safe.

Although the Greeks and Romans lived pretty close together on the map and learned a lot from each other and did many things alike and looked a lot alike, there the resemblance ends.

IN DAZE OF YORE

The Mayas in Mexico liked to live and sleep on high cliffs. They are extinct, of course.

The Dark Ages lasted until the invention of the electric light.

Among the fiercest fighters of the Medieval Period were the Visi gals.

Most of the writers of the Medieval Ages were illiterate.

Royalty wanted a system that made serfs stay on the royal land and work. It was a futile system.

The feudal system was a complicated way of preventing feuds among the mountain folks in Europe.

The English are descended chiefly from the Angels and Sextons.

The Duke of Normandy was able to cross the English Channel because of his large feet on which he carried thousands of fighting men.

Richard the Lion Hearted led the third charade.

The knights were called that because that is when they pulled most of their chivalry and other shenanigans.

Minnesingers traveled from town to town. They didn't sing too good, which is one reason they kept traveling.

Friars were short order cooks in monasteries.

When Martin Luther got especially mad he went around nailing bulls to doors.

Because of his heresy, Luther was denounced and restricted to a diet of worms.

Renaissance could not be pronounced in northern Europe until the sixteenth century.

Columbus claimed sailors could go east by going west. But then there are some people even today who claim that black is white.

Henry the Eighth often had the heads of his wives cut off and this was one of his worst merits.

Elizabeth could have saved Mary, Queen of Scots, if she would have just lifted her little finger. But she didn't. She was mean.

For centuries, Austria was ruled by a Hapsburg lion.

Following the Hapsburg line, Austria was next ruled by the line of Demarcation.

The French people have a Romantic Origin.

Marie Antoinette was killed, or rather had her head chopped off.

In a uniform or not, Lord Nelson was a dashing figure.

One cause of progress slowing up was when kings passed the power to their children and then on down to their children without letting the grownups run it.

After the French Revolution, General Upheaval took over. He did it in Paris.

One of the best values of history is learning what little they knew.

GENERAL CUSTARD AND JOHN WILKE'S BOOTH

To protect the North American Indians, the government put them in reservoirs.

History is getting longer and harder all the time.

When the Spaniards arrived in California, they considered the Indians to be heathens because none of the Indians could speak English.

The Pilgrims came over on the Mayfossil.

Along about then people started wearing bustles and looking for witches. I know it is crazy, but there was not much else to do in those days.

Before the time of George, Washington D.C was A.C.

The American revolution was caused by taxation without relaxation.

Doctors were so sparsely populated at that time it was a handy thing for the soldiers to know how to do respiration.

Thomas Jefferson believed in everybody's right to have four fathers.

George Washington never told a lie and I don't believe it.

The more I think about Aaron Burr, the less I think of him.

As John Paul Jones was sinking with his ship he remarked, "I have not yet begun to fight."

George Washington said no president should be sentenced to more than two terms in the Big House.

Benjamin Franklin went to France to get the support of the king of France and also his wife.

The Liberty Bell was probably named by Benson Lossing who was unfortunately cracked.

The Bill of Rights guarantees ten basic rights to ourselves and our posterior.

Colorado was first explored a long time ago. More people came. The sound of gold was heard shouted. Population was increased fast. Lewis and Clark were responsible for all this.

The reason the Louisiana Purchase was such a bargain was because we got so many more states than just Louisiana.

While exploring for the federal government in 1806, Zebulon Pike discovered the Peak that bears his name. Even today the Zebulon is a famous Peak few people have ever seen.

According to the Mexican War Peace Treaty, Mexico seeded all of California. Thanks to them for the big trees today.

One reason the South lost the war was because they kept making Confederate money, not knowing it was worthless.

Abraham Lincoln was sitting in a theater booth when he was killed. It was John Wilke's booth.

Lincoln's life teaches us the advantage of enjoying what we have, even if there isn't any.

Probably the fiercest Indian warriors were from the Apathy tribe.

Little Big Horn sounds as confusing to me as to General Custard.

Every U.S. soldier was trained to be brave. If he was scalped, he was never to show it.

The invention of the handcar made it possible for us to travel by hand as well as by foot.

The greenbacks were in favor of making all money legally tender.

The stage coaches carried people. The pony express carried ponies.

Rawhide saddles made people feel that way.

Under the Alien and Sedition Act, Aliens had to register their Seditions at the nearest post office.

Taxes on certain goods have come to be known as excite taxes.

Warren Harding got mixed up in all kinds of graft and corporation. So I'm not voting for him next time.

1929 was experienced by the whole world.

It was October 1929 when it finally happened. With the crash of the markets, valuable stocks became invaluable overnight.

Unfortunately the Depression happened just when everybody was out of work.

SOCIAL SCIENCE SIMPLIFIED

Gracious living is when somebody says the cost of living that way and somebody else says "Gracious!"

If a gentleman has etiquette, he will let the lady walk on the inside of his arm.

It used to be that people got mixed up about who owned what and got into fights. Today we have civilized lawyers to do it.

It is bad manners to break your bread and roll in your soup.

"For the benefit of mankind" means to think of your children. Or if you don't have any, then those children's children and theirs and on as far as you can think.

Many law enforcing officers say that walkers should be given tickets just like drivers when they disobey the law. It is for their own safeness. I hardily agree.

To have faith in your convictions means no matter how many times you go to jail you know it's for your own good.

Sublimation refers to a strange quirk of nature in which people have dogs instead of children.

Inflation is what we find in inferior tires and money.

Free capital goods are things you don't have to pay for like air for your tires or for you.

An invoice is your mathematical conscience.

Barter is when you buy things without money. I'm for it.

Whenever a bank pays you interest this is known as the divid end.

Income tacks are the most expensive kind.

We use pounds to measure fat but England uses them to measure money.

Money is valuable only from the standpoint of economics.

Stocks and bonds and all those things are not necessary. Many people have struck it rich with little more than money.

Inflation means that 10 pennies are now worth only one dime.

Patriarchate says your mother should be a he.

A peace treaty is an agreement that two countries won't fight until one does.

It takes an act of Congress to promote a brigand general.

America has an unusually large dairy industry with about five million farmers giving milk.

Some of the best products of Nevada are silver, fun and Kit Carson.

Much of the Middle West's grain goes to market in the form of beef. I was absent the day you explained how they do this.

Switzerland is quite rank in the production of cheese.

Chile is such a prosperous country that her exports are exceeded only by her imports.

Every ten years we count our censes. Five the last time

Post offices often mark over our stamps so we can't possibly use them again. This is a good example of the government waste we hear about.

Only in wars and epidemics does our country ask us to bear our arms.

A whereas is a legal paper.

Under the American system, economy sizes are big in soap flakes and small in cars.

The three branches of government are land, sea and air.

FOR CAMPAINS, TAKE TWO ASPIRANTS EVERY FOUR YEARS

Issues are when they tell what they advocake and what they don't.

The worst thing a candidate can do is to be told about a mistake he is making on some issue, but then keep on making the same mistake over and over, etc., etc., etc.

Candidates need to show more carefulness in their statements and their promises and their et se tras.

One good value of election campaigns is they let us know what problems we should be worrying about. And if we are not worrying, why we should be worrying.

Thin skinned is good in apples but bad in candidates.

Candidates are found in many sizes, shapes and meetings.

A minor party is one that people under 21 are allowed to join.

The Republicans and Democrats are the mainest parties in the United States.

Minority parties are called third parties. There are about 30 third parties in all.

Political ties are just to get elected and not to wear.

If I was at a convention, I would make a stiffly worded speech about how the candidates should think more about we lay-children even though we cannot vote for them.

During the demonstrations, a sea of humanity floods the isles.

The job of delegates is to resent their states.

When they talk about the most promising presidential candidate, they mean the one who can think of the most things to promise.

Political strategy is when you don't let people know you have run out of ideas and keep talking anyway.

Splinter groups are things that get in bandwagons.

A dark horse is a candidate that the delegates don't know well enough to dislike yet.

One of the strictest rules is all dark horses running for president must be people.

Noncommittal is to be able to talk and talk without saying anything.

Being nominated means watch out unless you don't mind being elected.

The people who are expected to help the president sometimes are locked up in his cabinet.

The campaign manager must have a smart head up his sleeve.

When a presidential candidate visits a city, the police stretch an accordion along his way.

The trouble with candidates is I don't understand everything they say. Like sometimes they say words with four or five cylinders.

Political slogans are brief unnecessary sayings.

A candidate should renounce his words carefully.

Having the privilege to vote is so important it is just to appreciate, not to really understand.

We have a White House. We have a president for it. Thinking about who is to be it is one of our constant doings.

I have found candidates to be extra talkity people.

Constituents are what people are except they can be chickens or anything you can get to vote for you.

An improvised speech is to pretend like he is just now thinking of what to say.

Thanks to democracy we now know that when a person votes he is somebody and not just a person because democracy teaches us everybody equals everybody else if they are Americans.

Politician is the bawling out name for a candidate you don't like.

Campaigns give some people a great deal of happiness by their finally ending.

People get to vote but computers get to say who will be president.

It may work for other choosings, but eeny meeny miney moe is not a good way for president choosings.

Many of our presidents have been people who were born right here in America.

Political science is to try to figure out what makes candidates act that way.

Once I was elected president. I was elected president of my third grade class only I did not know what to do about it.

The campaign is when the candidate tells what he stands for and the election is when the voters tell if they can stand for him being elected.

A split ticket is when you don't like any of them on the ticket so you tear it up.

Elections are made for exciting waitings.

We are learning how to make our election results known quicker and quicker. It is our campaigns we are having trouble getting any shorter.

A squeak-in is about 50 votes more than a neck-and-neck.

Also-ran means *goof* in the language of politics.

Some of our presidents never did much else and are famous only because they were presidents.

When the radio mentions a landslide, cross your fingers and hope it is talking about an election.

Calling a person a runner-up is the polite way of saying you lost.

Heredity is a bad thing in politics because it gets us kings instead of presidents.

After the winning candidate is elected, he is inoculated.

Even after a person is elected, he must concentrate and remember to be there on his
swearing-in day.

Before taking office, the president must raise his right hand and take some oats.

In January the president makes his acceptance speech after he has been sworn at.

Once he is elected, sometimes the president has to work 24 hours a day until he finds out what he is supposed to do.

Whatever else he does, a president isn't a very good president unless he sees to it that peace rages near and far.

AROUND THE WORLD
IN A NUTSHELL

Geography is good because it lets us go places. Even if we had already been there it is still fun. Once I visited Mexico and thanks to geography I can visit it again if I ever want to.

Atlantis is world famous for being lost.

Most of the Atlantic Ocean is somewhat below sea level.

Australia is located in the Pacific Ocean. It is presently still floating.

In Egypt, it is the custom for the gentlemen to wear turbines on their heads.

Greece is just a little spot on the map.

The two most important things a navigator should remember are where he is and where he wants to go.

A straight line is the shortest distance between two places unless you are flying with Lindbergh to Paris. Things are different there.

It used to be thought that we had 48 states in America. Then someone counted again and there was 50.

There is hardly any winter in Miami. They passed a law or something.

More people live in Road Island than is possible.

Although America is spread rather thin in other places, it is good and thick in the Rocky Mountains.

Denver has an elevation of about a mile. The elevator that makes this possible is one of the sights worth seeing.

Some parts of the Grand Canyon are a mile deep and two miles high.

The Antarctic is like the regular arctic, but ritzier.

A desert is a place where nothing is really there and everyone just sees mirages.

No one has ever seen the international date line because it is lost somewhere in the Pacific Ocean. But scientists are still looking.

The earth revolves on its axles.

Latitude makes it possible to have imaginary streets around the world without having to spend the money to build them.

Finland is called the land of the midnight sun because the sun can rise but can't set there. This is because Finland is so far east.

In many parts of the world, rainfall is so slight food will not grow unless it is irritated.

Europe has proved to be very useful in the study of geography.

The globe comes to a point as you reach either pole because everything shrinks in the cold.

The bottom of the ocean is covered mostly with ooze, gush and goo.

Holland is a low, lying country.

Colombia is both mountainous and jungleous.

Panama was built to have something through which the Panama Canal could run.

When Richard Byrd went to the North Pole, he discovered Pole Bears, seals and little pieces of America.

Little America was discovered by an admirable bird.

A compass is useful to tell you how bad lost you are.

We live in the temperate zone. Torrid and frigid people live elsewhere.

The higher up we go, the lower the temperature gets. Some day I will figure this out.

Naughtical miles tell how far it is to places we should not go.

Canada and Australia have several things in common. For one they are both in the Common Wealth and for another they are both far apart.

If you keep going straight ahead some say you will just end up where you started! This is why some people think the earth is round. Actually it is round for a very different reason.

THE BEST THEY IS IN ENGLISH

Although I am rather weak in biology, I am the best they is in English class.

There is a difference between being able to talk orally and writtenly.

Whom is an uppity form of Who.

Can means we can do anything we want to and nobody is going to stop us, and *May* means maybe we better ask anyway.

When you are I, he, she, or they, you are in the subjective and are doing things. But when you are me, him, her, or them, you are in the objective and they are doing it back to you.

Good punctuation means not to be late.

A period is used after making a true statement. If it is impossible to believe, use an exclamation point

Sometimes punctuation marks all speak of the same thing, like !@#$%^&* are all saying *darn it.*

Compounds can be studied in either chemistry or sentences.

A period is to let the writer know he has finished his thought and he should stop thinking if he would only take a hint.

Remember not to use commas, when they are unnecessary.

"Don't" is a contraption.

Here is some English to be known. Whom instead of who. Never ain't. Diagraming also.

I am sort of unsure about sing, sang and sung. If I do it right now I know it is that I sing. But if I did it say yesterday I am not sure what I did.

Most words are easy for me to spell once I get the letters right.

Proper nouns are names you can call people in public.

An adverb is a word that you can't figure out anything else it could be.

Adjectives mortify nouns and pronouns like you and me.

To show possession, you should use a positive s.

A biography is the life story of a person while an autobiography tells about his car.

! and ? and : are all useful for puncturing a sentence.

Parenthetical expressions are things mothers and fathers are always saying.

To write a story in the first person means to write it like Adam would.

Before you decide between using the words *bring* or *take* try to find out if you are coming or going.

Anyone that says *not* and *no* in the same sentence is really saying *yes*. And that goes for *n't* too.

Some of the up and ups claim Aesop didn't write anything and might not have even lived! That's a lot of hooey. They ought to have their head examined because I personally have read some of his fables and can vowch for him.

BODY BONERS

Our inherited traits are carried in our jeans.

Laps are so that more than one person can sit on a chair at the same time.

There are 26 vitamins in all but some of the letters are yet to be discovered. Finding them all means living forever.

The humorous vein supplies blood to the funny bone.

Sound would not be all that important to study if it was not for ears.

There are cavities all through our bodies. Don't worry because that is all right as long as they don't get into our teeth.

Germs are so small because things like penicillin scrunch their growth.

Skin is used to help hold people inside themselves.

Without red cells, blood would bleed to death.

The head is attached to the top of the back bone. This makes it more convenient.

The brain sits in the seat of consciousness.

When people are just skeletons, they are still themselves but their looks are gone.

Bones are what keep us from being too floppy and relaxed.

It is thought by most that there is only one heart for each of us. But I am thinking we may soon find others. I myself have felt them in my wrist and head for two more. Some day others may find these and other places.

The brain is what tells everything else to get busy and do around.

Without ears I would not be able to hear all the sounds I hear like WHOOOooo. Gik Gak. Eeeeaaaooo. FLIBIFLABOS. flibiflabos. Sometimes I am glad I have ears.

Hearts are useful for valentines and causing people to marry.

The Brain does not tell us to breathe. What tells us is the Instinct, which nobody knows where it is located.

Going down our human neck we find the sacoughagus, telling us when to cough.

The trachea is an air conditioning tube.

Digestion is done best on an empty stomach.

A calorie is the heat needed to raise the temperature of one gram of water one degree. People count their calories so they won't boil over.

Blood keeps going because the heart is always pushing on it and never lets it rest. I have known some people like this.

Most doctors can tell about your heart by using their horoscopes.

We humans are both vertebrates and mammals. You see we are smart enough to know how to be both at the same time.

Without lungs the body would not get the fresh air it needs to live. So the lungs are on our side.

When you are standing, the tibia is just north of the fibula.

In George Washington's time, they believed in "bleeding" sick people. Today we know to give them blood plaster.

Standing on your legs too long gives you very close veins.

If anybody cut his leg real bad, I would take it to the nearest doctor.

Ancestors are important. Without them you probably would not have had a mother or father. Everybody ought to have an ancestor.

The well rounded person is made up of both brains and bronze.

I have been vaccinated for all the childish diseases.

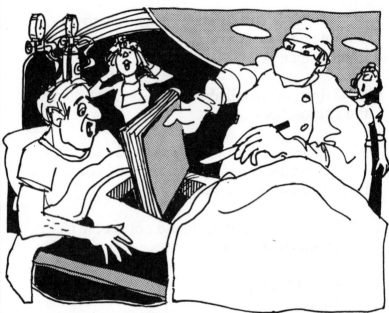

An appendix is something found in the back of a book. Sometimes they get in people and have to be taken out.

There are several ways to give artificial respiration. It might be best to ask the victim which way he wants it.

Nerves are what we need to get messages up to the brain . And they let you face anybody and be brave.

Although I weigh 88 pounds, I weigh only 40 kilograms. Just because, I guess.

THE JOY FEELS OF MUSIC

Music gives me joy feels all over.

Probably the most marvelous fugue was the one between the Hatfields and the McCoys.

If you keep moving two fingers real fast on the piano, you get a thrill.

Kettle drummers have copper bottoms that look like round kitchen pots. Their skin can be stretched to have them make high or low sounds.

Most good singers have at least a two octane range.

The lowest noted strung instrument is the bass vile.

An oboe is a woodwind, whatever that is.

Sharps are skinny and flats are fat.

Flats are okay in music but bad in tires.

A 32nd note is only just a little molecule of music.

Good singers nauseate their words clearly.

Notes wouldn't be anything without music.

Minor keys are those allowable for children-composers under eighteen.

A trumpet is an instrument when it is not an elephant sound.

The English horn is like having a clarinet mother and an oboe father.

While trombones have tubes, trumpets prefer to wear valves.

A bassoon looks like nothing I have ever heard.

The main trouble with a French horn is that it is too tangled up.

Has anyone else ever made music on a waste basket, or am I the original composer?

A triangle can make the quietest noise I ever heard.

An English horn sounds like the gray light time of day.

Anyone who can read all the instrument notes at the same time gets to be the conductor.

The most dangerous part about playing cymbals is near the nose.

My favorite instrument is the bassoon. It is so hard to play that people seldom play it. That is why I like the bassoon best.

It is easy to teach anybody to play the maracas. Just grip the neck firmly and shake him in rhythm.

Just about any animal skin can be stretched over a frame to make a pleasant sound once the animal is removed.

The harp has to vibrate to all the strings it has because of the shape it is in.

I saw one marching band last fall that wasn't very good. Its lines were all wrinkled.

The difference between a violin and a fiddle is about $1000.

The music I like best is Peter and the Wolf because it does things most music cannot do such as chirp-chirp, quack-quack and grrrr.

While I was listening to Tubby the Tuba I didn't laugh, but I grinned underneath.

Go Tell Aunt Rhody will be my favorite song when I am old and in a remembering mood.

The chief value of The 1812 Overture is to help remember the date.

A ballet is like a short ballad except they sing it while they stand on their toes. This keeps it short.

My favorite composer is Antonio Vivaldi. I am looking forward to hearing some of his music some day.

Johann Christian Bach was Johann Sebastian Bach's son. Otherwise they were unrelated.

Johann Sebastian Bach died from 1750 to the present.

Haydn and Mozart were friends at first but later became contemporaries.

When Mozart couldn't get a job in a royal court, his bread and butter was cut right out from under his feet.

Beethoven wrote music even though he was deaf. He was so deaf he wrote loud music.

My very best liked piece is the Bronze Lullaby.

Johann Strauss, Jr. wrote *The Merry Widow*. Oh. The music not the lady.

Felix Mendelssohn seems to have been happy, honest and well liked, although a musician.

Wagner's music is made for triumphs.

Carmen is an opera that has everything a good opera should have, such as actors.

I practice my piano every day unless it is rainy or sunshinny.

I wasn't nervous when I sang in the Christmas program. Just my knees were.

When a singer sings, he stirs up the air and makes it hit any passing eardrums. But if he is good he knows how to keep it from hurting.

Contralto is a low sort of music that only ladies sing.

Most authorities agree that music of antiquity was written long ago.

One of the sections of the orchestra is the concussion section.

I can't reach the brakes on this piano.

Pizzacato is a trick only string instruments know how to do.

A tuba is much larger than its name.

TURTLES LIKE GOOEY BEDS

The home for a turtle should have two inches of dirt in it with three inches of water. Don't worry because turtles like gooey beds.

We should be kind to our animal friends. We should chase and wrestle and toss them around so they will know we love them.

Dinosaurs kept humans extinct until much later.

Some dinosaurs had the presents of mind to step into a tar pit for preservation.

If you see a ewe you do not see you, you see a sheep.

When the frogs are in the water as tadpoles, they get in a bad habit of eating their own tails. Only on land is a frog safe from eating hisself up.

Otters have more fun than most anybody else.

A marsupial is an animal that carries itself around in its pouch.

Penguins are birds. Sure they don't fly, but they can't fool me.

Flycatcher birds use snake skins in their nests. I might mention this is after the snakes are through wearing them.

The road runner is not as flighty as most birds.

The down feathers keep birds from flying
 too high.

I had a pet parakeet but it got out and a cat ate it
so the cat's my pet now.

Alligators like to hatch out of eggs just like birds.
I hate when they try to be something they aren't.

To learn the sex of a chicken, you can look at the
egg to get no hint at all.

I understand how the chicks get out of their
shells, but how they get in who knows.

The platypus would be a mammal except he lays
eggs. This isn't too bad a thing so I vote to let
him go ahead and be a mammal.

A setter is a dog that is only good at one thing.

Dogs age much quicker than people. In less than
two months they are a year old.

When animals seem to be thinking, they are
usually only instincting.

You should always say octopi when you mean
there are two or more octopuses.

We used to depend only on silkworms until we
noticed rayonworms and nylonworms.

A silkworm has not 1 but *tee-double-U-oh!* holes in his head. Instead of sitting and sulking he uses them to make silk.

Caterpillars are made of fuzz and squash.

If fish could be mammals, the sea horse would be the first to do it.

Butterflies are worms at first. But then they learn right from wrong and change to butter-fly ways.

It is the male that says, "Katy did!" He has to hang upside down and rub his wings together, but it is worth it to him.

SOME TREES
JUST STAND AROUND

Some trees give us berries or cherries or plums. Others are content to just stand around and add rings.

A hybrid is a thing that is not its own self.

All trees are either evergreen or broadleaf. If you are a tree, you have to make up your mind.

Cotton is used to make clothes and gin.

One thing I learned about trees is that they can teach their leaves how to make food. They're not so dumb.

A tundra is a vast treeless forest.

One of the prettiest but saddest sighted trees is the weepy willow.

In the fall it is called that to let the leaves know what to do.

Many plants have been named after animals such as foxgloves, tiger lilies and dandy lions.

Climbed trees are to make kids happier.

The sunflower comes from the same family as the dandelion. We know that many families have at least one black sheep.

Seeds should be buried whether they are dead or not.

In winter most trees get bald.

Many of our weeds need some form of birth control.

Egg plants are where baby chicks think they come from.

Grass seed gives us more grass, but bird seed doesn't give us more birds.

Last December I learned a song about the kissletoe.

Our lawn has crabby grass.

I NEVER GET SLEEPY
IN MY SEANCE CLASS

Some of my classes are boring, but I never get sleepy in my seance class.

The scientific method is not to believe anyone until you find it out for yourself.

Scientific knowledge is knowing things like how to make time go backward by the B.C. method.

Once I saw some germs scrunched together in a pond water drop. Pond water germs are very interesting folks. All their ways are herky ways and jerky ways.

Science class is where we learn how tomorrow happens.

Scientists have now invented watches that can run on either standard or daylight time.

A scientific assumption is a fact so simple we do not need to understand it.

For some reason, when I looked in the microphone I could not see anything.

A scientific hypothesis is something you assume to be true even though you and everybody else knows it isn't.

A scientific miracle is something that cannot happen until it does.

Living things of our own time have not yet had time to turn to fossils. People in science are waiting anxiously so they can study them also.

An archaeologist is an excavated prehistoric ruin.

Fossils are dug up by archaeologists.
If dogs dig them up we call them bones.

Many of the dead animals of the past changed to dirt or oil while others decided to be fossils.

BRAVE NEW ELECTRONIC WORLD

Think of a volt. Wow! Because now you have had the same thought as Voltaire, after who this thought was named.

Electronic music sometimes sounds like a rocket blasting itself off to adventure.

A radio telescope is a thing you can hear programs by looking through it.

When we take the electricity and push and squeeze it up through the wires, we like it a lot because it is serving mankind. How much the electricity likes it is unbeknownst.

Electronics is the study of how to get electricity without lightning.

Voltage tells the age of electricity.

Electricity is a stream of electricians running through a wire.

The Hoover Dam holds ten quarts of water for every one quart of electricity.

See there are these electrons and protons that are on opposite sides of the atom. They meet and fight it out. When things get hottest and the atom can't stand it any more, it explodes.

I think I admire the electron more than anything else about the atom because it weighs only about one over 2000th as much as a proton but can still hold its own.

WHAT WATT!

There are some things about electricity we still are not sure of. These things are called whats.

In finding out that light bulbs heat, the fun is not in the fingers.

Electrons carry the negative charge while the protons provide the affirmative.

HISTORY ON THE ROCKS

When any place is going to have an earth-quake, guess when it will be? That is as good a guess as anybody's since no one knows for sure.

Men who know how figured out that if Mt. Everest was thrown into the deep downmost part of the ocean it would all be under water, so we know not to go to all the trouble of throwing it in there.

To have an earth you must first get your thunder roaring and your earthquakes shaking and your volcanoes spouting. It is a noisy business to become an earth you see.

California will be completely under water in a few million years. Just wait and see.

Rumor has it that many caves have monsters living in them. These monsters are called spelunkers.

What lodestones are loded with are magnets.

As hard rocks grow older they change into soft soil. The first hundred years of a rock's life are the hardest.

A rock weighs less under water in case I ever want to know.

Granite is made in a deep fire under the earth. I think you can guess who makes it.

It is against the rules to pick up a
Petrified Forest.

The ocean stores its extra water on its
continental shelf.

Water can wear away a rock until it is completely
unvisible. But don't expect it to happen in one class
period.

If wind and water and weather did not break
rocks down, the balance of nature would soon
be destroyed.

Geysers are like us humans and have to let off steam sometimes.

Quicksand is either watery sand or sandy water but it is too dangerous to really find out which.

I know all rocks are very old. I do not know what they were as children.

When a volcano erupts, what it erupts mostly is larva.

There is a tremendous weight pressing down on the center of the earth because of so much population stomping around up here these days.

Rock is what you call all of them you don't know the exact name for.

Sand is found in both hot deserts and cool seashores. It can grow anywhere.

Geologists are interested in the earth's beneath.

The earth has a tremendous gravitational pull, but thanks to science we have learned to live with it.

Dinosaurs knew how to make oil. The secret died with them.

Unlike most things, rocks start big and gradually get littler. They are of a backward growth, you see.

We can call crude oil "crude" if we want to, but just don't forget how we depend on it.

Volcanoes give us hot java.

Now that dinosaurs are extinct, we can safely call them clumsy and stupid.

Oil is formed by the process of waiting.

Earthquakes are caused by horizontal up and down movements, giving an unsteadying effect to everything.

Talc is found in rocks and on babies.

I used to think there was only one kind of drawing. Like with a pencil. But now I know things can also be drawn the magnet way.

Gravity is what pulls things together. There is a great deal of gravity in magnets.

The law of gravity says no fair jumping up without coming back down.

One of the best things they found in magnesium is magnets.

Basalt rock is also igneous rock. People have two names and so can it.

Copper ore is spelled o-r-e so no one will try to row with it.

Gravity is with us most in the fall.

We call a small rock pebble and we call a big rock bolder. Being bigger, they are.

Some rocks have bands in them. The streaky kind. No music.

Basalt does not, as you might think, taste as you might think it might.

Oxygen is for burning or breathing depending on whether you are rockets or people.

In making water, it takes everything from H to O.

The secret spelling for water is H2O.

The earth holds on to everything with its grabity.

Even in ancient times some people guessed the earth was round, but the more intelligent knew better.

The very center of the earth has irons in it. These big irons are what keep the center of the earth so hot.

Scientifically, some forests are called petrified. Diggingly, they are called rocks.

In the deepest parts of the oceans there are many mountains. But nobody has been able to climb to the bottom of these mountains.

Some rocks are made under water. It gives the water something to do.

SOME CHEMICAL REACTIONS

Say you have some nitrogen. That is all right.
Say you mixed it with glycerin. Then don't
say I didn't warn you.

Glycerin is a sweet oily BOOM!

A fire must have oxygen, but not too much.
Giving it too much is known as blowing
it out.

Hydrogen is a bombious gas.

Iron is very useful unless it meets oxygen.
Then it is rust. It is like a person getting in
with the wrong crowd.

One of the most useful by-products of fire
is heat.

If you put a piece of copper in a hot flame, a
powder starts forming on it. This is the way
copper says "Ouch!"

Only 21% of the air is oxygen. Every time we
burn a fire it takes oxygen. For the sake of our
remaining oxygen, we should not start any
more unnecessary fires.

Fire and combustion are much alike except fire
burns things down while combustion burns
them up.

The best thing carbon monoxide is good for is running away from.

Oxygen can be burnt. Engines know how to do it.

After chemists went to all the trouble to learn how to mix iron and oxygen, they only came up with rust. So it does not pay to get too fancy.

One way to tell for sure if a sweater is made of wool is to hold it over a flame. If it burns slowly it is wool.

Another name for fire is oxidation, but I think I will just stick with the first name.

Alkaline can cause red litmus paper to turn blue. As far as I know, this is its only talent.

Some unscruplus men have made aspirin and other medicines out of old coal tar!

There is nothing to keep a liquid from changing to another state. The Mississippi River, as we all know, does not have to stay in that state alone.

To most people solutions mean finding the answers. But to chemists, solutions are things that are all mixed up.

In looking at a drop of water under a microscope, we find that there are twice as many H's as O's.

Water is the most common of everything we see.

Coal is made from sand and dead plants. Or if you will wait a few million years you can have a diamond.

Iron is dry rust.

Liquid fuels, such as gasoline and oil, explode quicker than any other kinds. But we carelessly continue to use them in our own cars.

Water really has oxygen just like we breathe, but don't try it.

I think you said flammable means inflammable. But now I forget which both means.

If you pour acid on metal you get itchings.

A spectroscope is a thing used to study specks.

Some oxygen molecules help fires to burn while others choose to help make water, so sometimes it is brother against brother.

Cyanide is so poisonous that one drop of it on a dog's tongue will kill the strongest man.

Some people use salt to freeze ice cream while others use it to melt snow. One day we will see who is right.

With all the uses to be made of rubber it was necessary to find a substitute. After all, rubber does not grow on trees.

Chemistry was begun by alchemists who were looking for gold but had to settle for chemistry.

Formula is the language that chemists speak.

Physical chemistry is what you get from mixing physics and chemistry together.

The word for "trinitroluen" has been changed to TNT so people that read it can get started running earlier.

FISSION + FUSION = CONFUSION

Before a rocket can go into space, it must get through the earth's gravy.

A rocket has no moving parts. Except itself. Straight up.

Liquid fuel rockets will not go unless they have both a fuel tank and an oxidizer tank. And don't forget the match.

In order to go straight, the rocket fuel must burn even. Even what is a military secret.

Molecules all pull together. They have learned the value of sticking together. Because of this, even though they are very tiny, molecules will probably never become extinct.

Here is how to prove there are molecules. First look at a whole pile of sand. Next look at each separate grain of sand. Now that we have proved that we can go on to another experiment.

Heavy water is like with ships in it.

If you are in a boat and want to stop, the best way is to dig your pole in the bottom of the river. Friction can always stop you this way even if the boat goes on.

Molecules move. It is true! (Behind our backs, of course.)

Molecules are constantly bumping into each other in the air. There is really quite an overpopulation of molecules.

While molecules in gases and liquids bounce around from place to place, in solids they just lie there and vibrate.

The hotter anything gets, the faster the molecules in it move. Like if a person sits on something hot, his molecules tell him to get up quick.

When they broke open molecules they found they were stuffed with atoms. But when they broke open atoms, they found them stuffed with explosions.

A Geiger counter is a device used to count Geigers.

Centrifugal force is that force caused by moving bodies. It's all pretty spooky.

Gravity is a process that started in Isaac Newton and spread all over the world.

Isaac Newton noticed that anything at rest tended to remain at rest. For this he grew famous.

I plan to report on neutrons because of the important sound of their names.

Atoms are so small you could put a zillion of them on the head of a pin. P. S. There is not really as large a figure as a zillion. A zillion is only a figure of speech.

Sound travels better in water than in air because in water the molecules are much closer apart.

Atoms are what hold everything together. Atoms are a small but important occupation.

TORNADOES ARE A BIT TOO MUCH

The word thunderstruck means astonished. What makes the person so astonished is that only lightning is supposed to strike anybody.

The most violent of all large storms are the tycoons.

Although air is hollow, it is not just used for looking through. It is also good for breathing and trying to answer questions about.

Weather is like climate except for the difference that is yet to be found.

Too much wind causes typhoon fever.

The difference between air and water is that air can be made wetter but water cannot.

Drops that are carried up and covered with snow then down with water is the recipe for hail balls.

The top of a room's air is hotter than its bottom.

A weather vane will not tell you the weather. All it will tell you is the wind.

In order to have seasons, we had to get the earth tilted over on its axis. But it has been worth it.

Climate means hot or cold while weather means wet or dry.

Only the gases that are highest up get to be called atmosphere.

The higher the altitude goes, the thinner the air gets. Mountain climbers tell us it is much harder to breathe this skinny air.

Climate is with us all the time while weather comes and goes.

The wind is like the air, only pushier.

You told me warm air rises and then you said the higher you go, the colder it gets. Which may I believe?

Cyclones are caused by hot and cold running air.

Water vapor gets together in a cloud. When it is big enough to be called a drop, it does.

Rain is saved up in cloud banks.

Humidity is the experience of looking for air and finding water.

Meteorologists do not really get paid for studying meteors. What they do get paid for is anybody's guess.

We get our temperature three different ways. Either Fahrenheit or Celcius or Centipede.

When you mix water and air you get humidity.

We have soft water when it rains. We have hard water when it hails.

If there is cold air on top and warm air under-neath, everything starts pushing and shoving to change places.

100 humidities equal 1 rain.

We keep track of the humidity in the air so we won't drown when we breathe.

Clouds are what make the moon move when you watch it.

To think that snowflakes fall from the stars is crazy. We all learn that snowflakes have SIX points.

A blizzard is when it snows sideways.

Rain clouds float around up there and then bump into each other and out falls the rain.

The four seasons are the best ones I know.

We can expect rain most when the pressure is feeling low.

The highest of all clouds are the circus clouds.

You can listen to thunder after lightning and tell how close you came to getting hit. If you don't hear it then you got hit, so never mind.

A water spout is a wet tornado.

Anyone interested in the weather might ask how clouds are made. I am not going to say for sure until I find out the answer.

The water cycle is a thing on which people can ride on the water by pedaling along. I don't believe it has been invented yet.

Air is called atmosphere when we want it to sound more dignified.

Sleet is rain or snow that cannot make up its mind which.

The more a humidity goes over 100%, the harder it rains.

The speed limit for gales is 75 miles. Above that they get called hurricanes and other bad names.

Thunder is the noise that air makes when lightning jumps through it. So would anybody.

When fog comes around, you might as well not mind looking at it.

Clouds are high flying fogs.

Rain is huddled and snuggled vapor.

A hurricane is a breeze of a bigly size.

The barometer tells us fair weather gives higher pressure that presses on us harder than rain. Common sense tells us something else.

Rain water has a plural known as thunderstorms.

Air also has an important purpose of filling up space. Here is a demonstration.
(.) When you are not saying anything on paper, what is being said is air!air!air! 100 times.

ASTRONOMERS ANONYMOUS

While the earth seems to be knowingly keeping its distance from the sun, it is really only centrificating.

All of outer space is a vacuum. Comets are like vacuum cleaners that sweep up the dust in the universe.

Most books now say our sun is a star. But it still knows how to change back into a sun in the day-time.

We make a new resolution about the sun every 24 hours.

Calculating astronomers say our sun will burn up in a few billion years. If everyone knew this there would be more church going.

The point where the moon is nearest the earth is the perily. The point fartherest from the earth is the apology.

It took our best astronomers to figure out how to cross an equine-ox.

A meteorite is a dead meteor.

The earth is only one of jillions of stars and is important only because some of us live here.

When things heaten they expand.
Our expanding universe, just as a case, is
caused by our increasing hot summers.

Mars is so far off it would take a million years to
walk there on an express train.

To anyone on the moon, they would look and think
the earth is only just a mirror for the sun, so that
shows how much they know.

One reason for getting to Mars is that people live
longer there. Say like a man is 100 years on Earth,
well he is much less older on Mars. It sounds crazy
but it is so.

There is one side of the moon most people have
never looked at. I am not sure exactly which
side it is.

The earth is moving through space at a terrific
speed, circling the sun while the moon circles us.
At least this is the latest theory.

The planets traveling around the sun are all part of
our Sonar System.

When we see the sitting sun at night it does not
really move. We are the ones that move and sit.

Night is when we get on the shady side of the sun.

The "moon" is really a satellite of the earth. But me
and a lot of other people still catch ourselves calling
it "moon."

Eclipsing is the way the moon has of telling us we are interfering with its sunlight.

Some people can tell what time it is by looking at the sun, but I have never been able to make out the numbers.

A trip to the moon takes longer than I would care to take the time to figure out.

Space scientists call outer space that. This is as good a name as I can think for it.

In order to know that the moon has gravity I need only look at the tides. Somehow this proves it to me conclusively.

Some claim that days and nights on the moon are two weeks long. This makes for good talk if nothing happened on the news.

The moon means more to us than the sun because it shines at night when we need it most.

The sun always gets to the Central Time Zone before the Mountain Time Zone because there are not so many mountains to climb.

Everybody leans to the sun in summer and away in winter. We are all a little tipsy that way.

The solar plexus is a star that is yet to be found.

Saturn is a planet we find located somewhere close to the universe.

The first person that actually orbited the earth was a dog.

While the sun continues to recklessly fly through space, we blindly follow along and around it. But some day we will learn how to go on our own and then watch out.

For many years people thought that Venus might be inhabited by women, dragons or other strange creatures.

There is a new moon every month, but we only say that. Really it is the same old moon every time.

The best influence the moon has had on the earth so far has been to stay out of our way.

We know much more than ancient people did. They thought it was 240,000 miles to the moon. We found out it was 240,000 miles. The difference is we KNOW.

It is 93 million miles from the earth to the sun as the crow flies.

The sun is really a star. How it fools us is by shining in the day and being of the unpointed kind.

The sun is constantly burning and the cinders show up as sunspots.

It takes the earth 24 hours to roll over.

The sun is much larger than I believe.

A planet cannot have an axis until it can get a lion to run through it.

For millions of years there was a sun but no earth. This kept mankind from making much progress.

The earth has been here a long, long time. But the sun has been there a long, long, long time.

Radiation belts help hold the sun's rays up.

Night and Day and Seasons are just a few of
the advantages of belonging to the
Solar System.

The axis is only a make-believe line, but somehow the earth manages to turn on it.

The two main creatures of outer space are
particles and vacuums.

Air is for breathing while atmosphere is for
talking about.

The atmosphere is a blanket when it is
not a gas.

The sun's crooked sunshine is slanted in the
winter but it gets straightened out in the sum-
mertime.

There is no air in space. That means there is
nothing. Try to think of it. It is easier to think
of anything than nothing.

The moon is a planet just like the earth only
deader .

We figured up that I would be five years older
if I lived on Venus. Everybody I know on
Venus lives faster.

The North Star, as a matter of fact, is almost
straight north. This is quite a coincidence.

A meteor is a piece of stone or metal passing through our celestial body. But it don't hurt.

The sun gives us heat and light. Most scientists claim the sun is rather important to us.

Between sun and moon comes the gray light time. When sunlight and moonlight is stirred up together, the shadows do have such velvety fingers.

The universe is bigger than most anything I can think of.

An orbit is a surrounded sun while a circle is a surrounded nothin.

For as long as the moon has been there, it has made a trip around the earth every month. There is not much else to do.

Gravity is stronger on the earth than on the moon because here on earth we have a bigger mess.

The brightness of novas in the sky catch our eye because they are bursting into 97 trillion pieces. They will do anything to show off.

The sun has to use about 4,200,000 tons of itself every second to keep burning, but that is what it enjoys doing best so oh well.

Some people think Neptune is a person that lives in the sea. Others think he is a planet. We know his name, but we can't find him.

Harold Dunn

Hardly a teacher exists who hasn't at least once regretted failing to write down the amusing statements and answers that come out of every classroom. Harold Dunn has few regrets in this regard. He *did* collect the gems that surfaced over his long career as a teacher in the elementary public schools of Gallup, New Mexico, and in Jefferson City and St. Louis County, Missouri.

Now retired, Dunn went into teaching because he "simply enjoyed children and the way they responded to their world." A former member of the first violin section of the Springfield (Missouri) symphony orchestra, he also enjoys gardening, and is especially interested in science and government.

He holds a bachelor's degree from Southwest Missouri State University and a master's from Baylor University. During his army service, he was stationed at White Sands Proving Ground, New Mexico in the First Guided Missile Battalion.

Having no children of his own, Harold Dunn thinks of the thousands of children he has taught as "family" and remembers the years he spent with them as being " far more fun than work, " a phrase that serves equally well to describe *The World According to Kids*.

GREAT GIFTS! LOTS OF LAUGHS! ORDER TODAY!

BOOK TITLE	AUTHOR	DESCRIPTION	ORDER NUMBER	QUANTITY	PRICE	TOTAL
1 Ways to Dump Your EX!	Oaky Miller	Getting even after divorce	0-930753-01-1		$5.95	
erAntics	W. J. Brooke	Hilarious operatic spoof	0-930753-02-X		$7.95	
ings To Worry out	Len Cellla	Zany worries and phobias	0-930753-03-8		$6.95	
e Grandparents' ok	A. & S. Little	The light side of grandparenting	0-930753-04-6		$6.95	
w To Speak New rkese	J. Levine & N. Jackson	Daffy definitions of a strange language	0-930753–07-0		$6.95	
pid Stories	R.J. Leonard	Utterly silly stories for smart kids	0-930753-05-4		$5.95	
ey're a Very ccessful Family!	J. Farris	New Yorker cartoonist views the "burbs"	0-930753-08-9		$6.95	
llege Slang 101	C. Eble	Undergraduates' underground language	0-930753-09–7		$5.95	
e Bumper cker Book	M. & D. Reilly	Highway humor in the fast lane	0-930753-10-0		$5.95	
ertime	V. Iovino	A coach's advice to over-zealous parents	0-930753-06-2		$6.95	
rink Wrap	P. S. Mueller	Wildly weird cartoons	0-930753-12-7		$6.95	
nkies	A. Denny	Short poems and long laughs	1-879865-01-7		$6.95	
re's Ronnie!	G. Melson	Nostalgic photo humor from the Reagan years	0-930753-00-3		$3.95	

				Subtotal	
Spectacle Lane Press PO Box 34 Georgetown, CT. 06829				Shipping and handling	
				Total paid	

Order from your local book store; or fill out and send this order blank along with ur check or money order for the total amount to Spectacle Lane Press, PO Box 34, eorgetown, CT 06829.

Add $2.50 shipping and handling for the first book and $.50 for each dditional book.

Add $2.00 more for books shipped to Canada. Overseas postage will be billed. low up to four weeks for delivery. Make check or money order

yable to Spectacle Lane Press Inc. Connecticut residents add state tax.

Quantity discounts available on request. Send book (s) to:

ame_____

ddress_____

ity_____State_____Zip_____

SPECTACLE LANE PRESS, INC.